WHEN SKIES AREN'T BLUE

A Physician's Personal Journey

ANDY LAURIE, MD

Published by Andy Laurie, MD
Cover and book design by Nicole Baron Designs

ISBN: 978-1-7364139-0-6 (paperback)
ISBN: 978-1-7364139-1-3 (e-book)
LCCN: 2021901166

DEDICATION

Watching someone you love ravaged by illness is perhaps the most painful journey of all.

To my mother and father, brother, children and most of all, my wonderful wife: I cannot imagine the pain you have all endured watching me suffer at the hands of this crummy disease. But remember, there will come an amazing time when the sky will always be blue.

Let's make sure we are all there to celebrate together!

CONTENTS

PREFACE

At the end of each of the *10 Powerful Steps*, you will find a prescription to put into practice when you are really struggling during those difficult times in life. I cannot begin to tell you the peace, comfort and emotional healing that these prescriptions will bring when your own skies aren't blue.

THE
JOURNEY
BEGINS

Cyndi and Andy's wedding day—1991

NOTHING BUT BLUE SKIES

I know there is no such thing as a perfect life. But gosh, mine was about as good as it gets. It was February of 2003. I was thirty-eight years old and just experienced the joy of my fourth child being brought into this world. Yeah, I was now a dad times four! The book of Psalms tells us that blessed is the person whose quiver is full, and my quiver was more than full. I certainly felt that blessing. A dad of four wonderful kids, truly amazing—check!

The Laurie kids (from left to right): Josh, Luke, Krista, and Becky

Cyndi and Andy in 2003
(photo taken a few weeks prior to the illness)

Cyndi and I had been married at that time for twelve years. I met her back in the summer of 1989. She was studying in the biomedical library at the UC San Diego Medical School. I had been a medical student for three years at the time and believe me when I say it was a rare site to see someone that attractive in that library. I was not about to miss my chance. So, I gulped hard, swallowed my nerves, and plopped my books down next to her to "study". That began a relationship with a truly incredible partner and soulmate. God has so blessed me with an amazing wife— check!

How about the career? People around the church sometimes get a little confused as they are not sure what to call me. Some just have a little fun calling me Doctor/Pastor Andy. You see, I have two careers. I am both a board-certified radiologist and an ordained pastor. I know it is an odd combination. But suffice it to say at that wonderful time in 2003, my two careers could not have been any better. As a physician, I was practicing as an emergency room radiologist covering several of the Emergency Rooms in Tucson, Arizona. It was a great job. There was never a boring shift; it was always exciting. Best of all, I was able to take those thirteen years of education after high school (four years of college as a biochemist, four years of medical school and five years of radiology residency) and use them to help those patients coming into the ER. I know many people do not necessarily enjoy going into work, but I really loved what I did as a physician—check!

As much as I enjoyed practicing medicine, my true passion in life was the ministry. As a physician, we can do our best to heal the body, but ultimately that healing is temporary. As a pastor, the difference that can be made is eternal. Nothing quite compares to it. It was 2003, and I was beginning my fifth year as a pastor at The Bridge Christian Church. We were preparing to launch a brand-new campus on the east side of Tucson. The church asked me if I would be willing to get that started. Are you kidding? Starting a brand new campus at one of the most successful churches in the city is a pastor's dream! It just did not get any better than that. Life as a pastor, amazing—check!

5

Check, check, check, and check! It was the spring of 2003 and my life was firing on all cylinders. I was busy for sure, juggling a family and two careers. But I had seemingly boundless energy. I was in perfect health. It was as good as it could get. Nothing but blue skies.

THE SKY TURNED DARK

Working as a physician covering emergency rooms certainly can inject a dose of realism into how one views life. Night after night I interpreted CT scans, MRI scans and ultrasounds of patients who woke up that morning having no idea that their life would forever be changed. There I was in the prime of my life, happy and healthy. And while I knew it was certainly possible that it could someday happen to me, I was still rocked when those storm clouds of failing health blew into my life.

It was December of 2003, and I had just celebrated my thirty-ninth birthday. Christmas was in the air at the Laurie house. Cyndi always worked hard to make Christmas special for the kids. Seven large stockings were hanging from the fireplace mantle; one for each of the kids, one for Cyndi, one for me, and of course one for the dog. The tree was filled with mostly homemade ornaments that Cyndi had from her childhood or others that our own kids had

7

made. Gingerbread houses clumsily but adorably deco-
rated by our children lined the counters. Stacks of Christmas cards, from our family and many friends from our
new church that I was pastoring, were on full display. The
smell of baking cookies permeated the house. It was seemingly the perfect Christmas—until the skies turned dark,
very dark.

I awoke the following morning thinking, *oh no I have
the stomach flu*. I was incredibly nauseous and throwing
up. Nobody likes that retching, queasy misery nausea
brings, but for me, even as a kid, I could never tolerate
it well. My poor mom
always had to put up
with my drama every
time I would get even a
little nauseated. This one

**It was seemingly the perfect
Christmas—until the skies
turned dark, very dark.**

was bad though. But I figured like stomach flus I had in
the past, I would just suffer through this for twenty-four
hours or so and it would pass. It did not. The throwing
up continued and by the third day I was so dehydrated
that Cyndi had to take me into the ER to receive IV fluids.
The overwhelming nausea and vomiting persisted for a
few weeks requiring more visits to the emergency room
and the need for IV resuscitation as my blood pressure
was becoming dangerously low. The ER doctors did not
have an explanation for what was going on, but were still
thinking it may be a lingering virus. After a month of
this misery, I knew full well there was something very
wrong. I had lost over twenty pounds and was struggling

to stay hydrated—struggling to stay alive. I needed some answers and quickly.

I had a friend with whom I did my internship who was a gastroenterologist in town, and I gave him a call and let him know what was happening with me. He was concerned, had me come in and began running numerous examinations: Endoscopy, ultrasound of the abdomen, CT scan of the abdomen and pelvis, MRI of the brain, HIDA study for gall bladder ejection function, extensive blood work and more. Everything came back negative. By this time, I was so weak I could hardly walk any longer. Something was seriously wrong; I was questioning how much longer I could even survive this and there were seemingly no answers from any of the doctors I had seen.

It was surreal. A few months prior I was healthy and vibrant, juggling two careers and raising four young kids. And now I was fighting for my very survival. Cyndi and I would spend hours together crying out to God for help—for answers. It was after one of those prayers that it "just so happened" I was reminded of something. I cannot begin to tell you how many times those "just so happened" moments occur with God. But it was after one of those crying out to God moments that I thought about a medical professor I had years ago. His name was Dr. Bill Johnson. I had not thought about him in well over a decade. I had only a single rotation with him

I cannot begin to tell you how many times those "just so happened" moments occur with God.

9

during my internship. But for some "just so happened" moment he came to my mind. I remember thinking he was one of the most brilliant doctors I'd ever worked with. He was a professor in the college of medicine and certified as both an internal medicine doctor and a gastroenterologist. He always seemed to have insight into those tricky patients that nobody could figure out. He was like a nice-guy version of the TV character Dr. House.

I had nothing to lose at this point. I looked up his number, said a quick prayer and gave him a call. I was stunned he remembered me given the years. But he did and when I explained to him what was going on, he said he would be glad to see what he could do. I forwarded him all my records, and a few days later he gave me a call and asked me to come to his office.

Cyndi drove me over to the university hospital for that appointment. We both knew I could not survive this much longer. We needed answers and this seemed to be our last hope. We prayed together and headed into that appointment. I remember the alarmed look on my former professor's face when he saw me. I was frail and weak, a shadow of that healthy young man he knew from the past.

I could not survive this much longer.

He took a detailed history and then did a physical exam. I do not think I will ever forget the moment that followed. He said, Andy I have looked over all your records and based on everything that I see, I believe I know what is happening to you. My heart froze as I clung to his every word. He said I had a disease in which my autonomic nervous system had stopped regulating itself normally. As a result, my entire gastrointestinal tract had basically shut down. He said there were only a few limited things he could try, but ultimately, I would need to go to the Mayo Clinic in Rochester, Minnesota, to get the care that I would need.

Cyndi and I wept. Not necessarily out of sadness. Not out of fear. But out of relief. At least we had an answer. We had no idea if there was any cure or anything to even help. But we at least knew what we were dealing with and were determined to do what it takes to get better. It was not easy to get an appointment at the Mayo Clinic. My condition was not common and there were not many doctors trained to deal with it. But eventually we got the appointment and headed off to Rochester.

The Mayo Clinic is an amazing facility. I trained at some of the best places in the country, but this was at another level. They ran numerous tests many of which were quite unpleasant to say the least. But when all was said and done, they confirmed the diagnosis that my former professor believed was going on. I had developed a failure of the autonomic system which had led to the shutting down of my GI (gastrointestinal) tract. I had so many questions. How did this happen? Is this permanent? Are there any cures? Is there anything to help me feel better? Patiently, they answered all those questions. They said that it is rare, but in someone like me, who was previously healthy, this was likely an autoimmune disease, which usually is triggered by a viral infection. And then the devastating news.

There was no cure. It was unlikely to resolve on its own. They could recommend things to help with the symptoms, but this was to be an ongoing issue.

I have found over the years of dealing with the ups and downs of this disease that hope is very fleeting. Hope is so easy to grasp onto and so easily destroyed. Over the next year, the Mayo Clinic came up with several combinations of different medications to try and help my gut to function better and to deal with the nausea. While there was some limited relief, certainly there was no cure and the nausea continued. I remember with each new medication I would get my hopes up thinking maybe this would be the one to finally take this awful nausea away. I would get my hopes up, only again to be crushed.

This roller coaster of emotions of hope and failed hope is one that so sadly defines much of the human condition in this broken world.

The Mayo Clinic was able to at least get me to a point where I could sustain myself at a basic level of functioning. However, the unrelenting nausea continued. Every morning when I woke up it felt exactly like the stomach flu to varying degrees. I was miserable, just miserable. While I could have probably survived that way for a while, I certainly did not want to live that way.

Hope is so easy to grasp onto and so easily destroyed.

So, it was recommended to me by an expert in my condition that I consider having a surgery in which they hooked electrical wires into the lining of my stomach and then charged it with a pacemaker battery. It was a new surgery, just recently FDA approved at the time, called an implantable gastric pacemaker. They said that it could potentially result in considerable improvement to the nausea. The surgery was not going to be an easy one and it certainly had its risks. But I was desperate, so I did it.

The surgery itself was a difficult one and in the end it did not improve the nausea much. Unfortunately, I ended up with an unexpected complication that turned my already significant illness into something much worse. Following the surgery, I ended up passing out and when I regained consciousness my heart was in a rhythm known as atrial fibrillation. This is an abnormal rhythm of the heart where the atria basically start contracting in a very erratic and rapid pace rather than the normal even sinus rhythm. The doctors were baffled as to why that happened to me without reason. My underlying heart was otherwise healthy. After about twenty-four hours, the atrial fibrillation spontaneously converted back to the regular rhythm. However, after that, every time I would stand up my heart rate would rapidly increase, and I would become very faint and lightheaded. It was so severe I would nearly pass out even while just trying to sit up straight, let alone trying to stand up. I was in dire condition and at a still young age had essentially become bed bound. I remember just lying in bed for countless hours with tears of frustration, devastation and disbelief over what was happening to me.

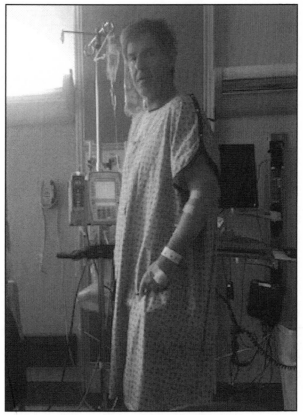

Hospitalized battling complications

I was being evaluated by an excellent cardiologist, Dr. Gregory Pennock, who I trained with during residency. He suspected that this was somehow related to the same underlying autonomic disease that impaired my gastrointestinal tract. He referred me back to the Mayo Clinic for more evaluation. Once again, after extensive and unpleasant testing they concurred that the same autoimmune process that attacked my gastrointestinal tract was going after my cardiovascular system as well. They postulated that somehow the surgery must have triggered it. So, I now had another devastating diagnosis to deal with: Postural Orthostatic Tachycardic Syndrome (POTS). This is a disease that effects that cardiovascular system in such a way that patients cannot regulate their heart rate and sometimes blood pressure in an upright position. Once again, it is something that has no cure and only limited medical therapy for treatment.

So, that is my story of how things turned dark in my life very quickly and permanently. I was now facing a life where every morning when I wake up, I battle symptoms that rival a stomach flu. It is now a life where the devastation of POTS makes even the most basic of tasks overwhelming, exhausting and sometimes impossible. It is a life where the norm is just feeling lousy. I was a young man still. I had four small children who needed their dad. I was still seemingly in the prime of my life. Yet, this now

I now had another devastating diagnosis ... POTS ... that has no cure ...

was my life. The blue skies had rapidly turned dark.

I have dealt with this devastating disease now for nearly two decades. I have been through so much on so many levels. And yet, I know my story is not unique to the human condition. As a physician and a pastor, I have seen the devastation that failing health brings to people physically, emotionally, and spiritually. And now as a patient, I personally understand that as well.

A Note From The Author

The reason that I embarked on writing this book despite my on-going health battles is because it is my hope and my prayer that what I have learned through this journey of illness will empower you or your loved ones to handle life when failing health has turned those blue skies dark.

What To Do

WHEN YOUR SKIES AREN'T BLUE?

10 Powerful Steps

When Skies Aren't Blue

WE NEED A HOPE THAT IS REAL

In the epic confrontation on Mount Carmel, the prophets of Baal passionately and fervently cried out to the most powerful of their gods for help and for victory. Their very lives were at stake. They would lose everything if their god did not come through for them. As much as they desperately needed their god and believed in their god and pleaded for their god's help; in the end: *"... there was no voice, no one answered, and no one paid attention"* (1 King 18:29). Their skies turned very dark and the heaviness of those words came crashing down as they realized their god was not real and their hope was crushed. The futility of a god that was not real was palpable.

If we are going to have the ability to persevere and even have victory when the skies in life turn dark, it is imperative that we know with certainty that our God is real. Otherwise, we too will feel the futility in those dark moments of *there was no voice, no one answered, and no one paid attention.*

The starting point of healing when our skies turn dark is understanding that our God is very real. When the skies are darkest in our life, it is not going to work to somehow just hope that God is true or wish that He is real—like some sort of fairy tale magic genie. At those moments we need to know! With 100% certainty, we need to know that God is real, and God is there for us regardless of what we are facing.

When I first became sick, my doctors ordered a CT scan of the abdomen. It showed there was some thickening of the wall of the stomach. There are many causes of thickening of the wall of a stomach on a CT scan. As a radiologist I knew one of the causes of a thick stomach on a CT scan is cancer. I also knew that if this were stomach cancer

The starting point of healing when our skies turn dark is understanding that our God is very real.

it was likely advanced and that I would not have long to live. Talk about surreal. I was thirty-nine years old. I had a family with four small kids who depended on me. I was in the prime of my life. I was healthy just a few months prior and now I could be dead in a short period of time. This was too overwhelming to even fathom. My gastroenterologist arranged to have a repeat CT scan. If the thickening was still present, then cancer was a very real concern. If the thickening was gone, then it was probably just some inflammation that had resolved. As I awaited that study, I contemplated the reality that I could shortly be given a death sentence. It is hard to fully describe all the emotions

I was dealing with. How did I handle that overwhelming moment? The first thing I did—I went back to faith 101! I pulled out a seminar booklet we did years ago at the church called "Facts Behind The Faith". This seminar provides the facts that prove God, Jesus and the Bible. It is beyond the scope of this book to go over all those facts. But suffice it to say, the facts are so compelling there simply is no question that God is real and the

How did I handle that overwhelming moment?... I went back to faith 101!

Bible must be true. So, I did a quick perusing of the book reminding myself that without a doubt: God is real, God is true, and God is still on His Throne, regardless of what I was going through. I was reminded of Psalm 46:1-3: "*God is our refuge and strength, a very present help in trouble. Therefore we will not fear, though the earth should change and though the mountains slip in the heart of the sea. . . .*"

I felt that comfort of God as He was telling me in this incredibly frightening moment: *Andy, I have got this one. I know this is overwhelming for you. But it is not too much for Me. Even if the worst of the worst should happen, I am your refuge and strength, I have got you.* I needed that. I could not just hope or wish that God is real, I needed to know. I was able to take that deep breath and move forward, knowing God will take me through this one way or another. This was not a fairy tale hope, but a rock-solid certainty. It is exactly what I needed.

Thankfully, it was not a fatal cancer. But that was one of many times that this disease has brought me to the

21

point of helplessness. It was one of many times that I have been so overwhelmed as those skies were darkened by this awful disease. It was one of many times that I had to bring myself back to the basics: God is real, and God's got this.

This certainly is not unique to just my situation. God created us and He understands that if our mind is constantly doubting, our faith will be weak and fail us. That is why God gives us so much proof. Think about how many times in scripture Jesus backed up His words with miracles to prove He truly is God. In John 10:38, Jesus said, *". . . believe the works, so that you may know and understand that the Father is in Me, and I in the Father."* His point was I am backing up My claims of deity with proof. The author of Hebrews reminds us of the very same thing *". . . how will we escape if we neglect so great a salvation? After it was at first spoken through the Lord, it was confirmed to us by those who heard, God also testifying with them, both by signs and wonders and by various miracles and by gifts of the Holy Spirit according to His own will"* (Hebrews 2:3-4). God never intended for us to believe on blind faith because He knew when our skies turned dark, we would need the confidence of not wishing, but knowing He is real and He is there for us.

God never intended for us to believe on blind faith because He knew when our skies turned dark, we would need the confidence . . .

I have to tell you it is that reality that drove me to become a Christian. When I was in college and in medical school, I honestly believed Christians were complete fools.

I believed they were intellectually weak and needed their fairy tale religion as a crutch to cling to. I had years of science behind me and there simply was no way I was going to believe in anything, let alone God, without facts. But once I took the time to study the facts out for myself, it became clear that I was the one who was being intellectually dishonest. The proof of God and the Bible is undeniable. It sometimes is an oddity to people that I have this dual career as a physician and a pastor. There is this thing in our culture today that says if you are educated in the sciences you could not possibly be a Christian. So, when people ask about why I chose the path I did, I think it surprises them when I respond it was the intellectual choice to do so based on facts. The look on their faces when I say that is priceless.

But that is the confidence God wants us to have. That is why He has given us an abundance of facts. It is both a powerful tool to draw people to Him and critical for us when our skies turn dark.

God says that He will "... *work all things together for good for those who love Him and are called according to His purpose*" (Romans 8:28). But that takes on a whole new sense of power when we understand that it is a factual statement. God says, *ok I understand that in this broken world sometimes the skies turn dark. But I am real, and I have proven it. I have got this thing. I can take even the darkest skies and work that together for good.*

Please understand I am not talking here solely about the power of faith and positive thinking. Positive thinking alone will not be able to overcome those dark sky moments in life. In medical school we were taught something known as the "placebo effect". The idea behind that is if a patient *thinks* they are receiving medication or therapy, then those

God can take even the darkest skies and work that together for good.

positive thoughts alone will help them in healing. And while there is an element of truth to that when it comes to therapy for medical illness, I can assure you

that does not work when life in this broken world smacks us to the ground. I mentioned Romans 8:28. This clearly says that it is God Who works all things together for good for those who love Him and are called according to His purpose. It does not say it is our belief that does it. It is not our faith that brings us comfort and healing; it is God Himself. When we know based on proof that God is true, that causes us to put our real faith in Him and live for Him (called according to His purpose). Then God steps in and brings us peace and healing even in the middle of the storm. It is through His power (not ours) that He works all things together for good. It is the beautiful combination of a rock-solid faith coupled with God's power that is the key. They both need to be in place.

Those provable facts of God are especially vital to avoid a spiritual spiral into darkness. There is a particularly devastating downward spiral that happens to our faith when our skies go dark. Here is the way it usually plays out. Things turn bad and our skies turn dark. Then, we stop thinking well and we do not process life well. When those skies turn dark, we naturally tend to question God and the reality of God.

Even as a pastor, I cannot tell you how many times that my failing health gets me down. That leads

It is the beautiful combination of a rock-solid faith coupled with God's power that is the key. They both need to be in place.

me to start doubting God. And I must keep reminding myself of those facts. If I do not, it becomes a vicious circle. The circumstances in our life bring us down. We then doubt God and that weakens our faith, which brings us down further, and our sky gets darker. I cannot stress enough how critical it is to break that cycle of negativity by knowing the facts that prove God and the Bible are true. You will constantly need to come back to them as you deal with those dark moments in life.

VICIOUS CIRCLE   VICIOUS CIRCLE BROKEN

One of my favorite passages reminding us of what powerful faith is all about is found in Hebrews 11:1. It tells us that "... *faith is the assurance of things hoped for and the conviction of things not seen.*" God is saying powerful faith is being sure of things you *can* prove, so that you can be confident of the things you *cannot* prove. We can be sure based on the facts that God is real, and God is true. And that means when your skies turn dark you can know with certainty that God is there working hard for you behind the scenes. That is the conviction of things not seen. It is this powerful faith built on provable truth that is critical for us to handle life when those skies turn dark.

So, get those facts! That is foundational. There are many resources available on-line. Some are better than others and you should do a bit of research. But I can personally say that both *Evidence That Demands A Verdict* and *More Than A Carpenter* by Josh McDowell are excellent resources. In addition, *The Case For Christ* by Lee Stroebel is also outstanding.

With just a little bit of reading and research, you can have all the facts you will need to develop a rock solid faith which will withstand even the darkest skies.

> *It is this powerful faith built on provable truth that is critical for us to handle life when those skies turn dark.*

I would like to share with you a spiritual prescription to help fortify that powerful faith in a very real and amazing God. It is a spiritual exercise that I do on a regular basis that is quite helpful when dealing with those dark sky moments. I take time in prayer and think about those things that cause me to be in awe of God. Sometimes it is just going out and looking at the stars in the sky. Sometimes it is looking at a spectacular

Tucson sunset. Sometimes it is pondering the complexity of life and realizing that the God Who created all this is real and provable and amazing. And *that* God is the same One I am now talking with in prayer. And *that* God loves me so much that He died for me. And *that* God is here, and He is real, and His heart is breaking, knowing His kid is hurting. And *that* God through His power will somehow take me through this. I cannot begin to tell you the peace, comfort and emotional healing that firmly knowing all of this will bring when your own skies aren't blue.

Author's Prayer

Father,
Thank you that you are so very real. You are amazing.
I know You are here, and You are listening. My skies are
dark now Father. But I know what is overwhelming for
me is not for You. So, God I ask You to be my refuge and
strength in this storm. I know You've got this.
And because You are real, I will not fear.
In Jesus' Name, Amen.

Rx PRESCRIPTION FOR WHEN SKIES AREN'T BLUE

Do these steps at least once a week during difficult times:

1) As you pray focus on those things that cause you to be in awe of God's power.

2) *Know* that the amazing God you are talking to in prayer is real.

3) *Know* that God loves you and died for you.

4) *Know* that God is with you right now and His heart is breaking for what you are going through.

5) *Know* that God in His love and His power will somehow take you through this.

Andy Laurie

ANDY LAURIE, MD

When Skies Aren't Blue

KNOW WHO DARKENED IT

It was past midnight. I was sleeping heavily when the sound of breaking glass jarred me awake. I went into the living room and was horrified at the site of complete destruction. The living room was ransacked. The TV and stereo equipment had been stolen. There he stood . . . right in front of me . . . the thief . . . the perpetrator. And I turned to him in shock and dismay and I asked him, *"will you please help me and bring me comfort in this difficult moment."* Huh? What? I turned to the perpetrator for help? That makes no sense. Nobody would do that. Yet, for many whose sky has been darkened in this broken world that is exactly what they end up doing. And, not surprising, it fails miserably. So, for us to take hold of the power of God when our skies aren't blue, we need to clearly understand who darkened it. We need to know who the perpetrator is and who is the hero.

So, let's look at the options here. Let's start with God.

Is God in any way responsible for the skies turning dark in our life? Is God causing those tragedies? Where is God in these dark sky times?

We need to know who the perpetrator is and who is the hero.

First, we need to make a clear delineation between skies that have been darkened because of poor choices we have made as opposed to those things that happen that are no fault of our own. The Bible is clear that there are things that God has said are harmful and wrong. God has said that if we choose to do them, they will mess up our life. The Bible calls those things sin. But simply stated these are the things that God says for our own good stay away from them; they will bring harm. When people make these destructive, sinful choices then absolutely there will be consequences and sometimes very painful ones that darken the skies of our life. God tells us there is that cause and effect with sin. In Numbers 32:23 He says, *"be sure your sin will find you out."* And sometimes it is actually God who is the author of those consequences. In Hebrews 12 it likens God to that loving dad who disciplines His kids out of a heart of love.

We need to make a clear delineation between skies that have been darkened because of poor choices . . . as opposed to those things that . . . are no fault of our own.

That discipline or those consequences are a loving dad's way to try and get His kids to get back to making those right and safe choices—

for their own good. The consequences of sinful choices certainly can lead to skies being darkened in our lives.

If this is your situation please understand God can work through these dark skies that you are facing. But the starting point to all of this begins with something that is not popular in our culture today . . . and that is repentance. Repentance simply means having genuine sorrow for what we have done and then going through that process of trying to fix it. Fixing it with God to start and if appropriate fixing it with others. Once you have gone through that process of genuine repentance then your journey to having God work on those dark skies can begin. And what you will learn in this book will be vital for you as you and God take this journey together.

Okay, but what about the bad that happens in life through no fault of our own? I can assure you that while I am not a perfect man, (only Jesus can claim that) I really do consistently strive to live my life for Christ. And when I do blow it (which we all will at times) I really do try and fix things with God and others. But, I have been and continue to be faithful to God as a pastor. I have followed God with consistency as a dad and a husband. I really was striving to do the right stuff when this awful disease struck. I remember so clearly when this illness hit that I carefully looked over my life to make sure there was no on-going sin that I was hiding or justifying. There was not.

Sometimes people can let themselves get a little freaked out over this one. They start over analyzing, thinking maybe there is this hidden sin, and that God is disciplining them.

But I am just not sure what it is? How can I get those dark skies cleared, if I don't even know what I am being disciplined for? Hmm, would God really do that? What kind of parent would that make Him? Can you imagine a parent who was disciplining their kid and their kid didn't even know what it was for? That would be abusive. That would not be the actions of a loving parent. God is the perfect loving parent in every way. When God disciplines us, we clearly will know what we are doing wrong and why our loving Father is doing it.

They start over analyzing, thinking maybe there is this hidden sin . . .

Whether we choose to respond and fix it or not is up to us, but we will know.

But, back to my situation, and one that much of humanity faces. Dark skies happen to those who are not doing wrong. Bad stuff happens to good people. In those cases, who is to blame? Is God the one doing it or allowing it? Who is the perpetrator? The answer for you and me is vital if we are going to have any chance of handling life when our skies turn dark.

So, let's look at the option that many people tend to believe: *God is the one doing this to me.* Is that possible? Is it consistent with the character of God? Is it consistent with the Bible?

While I was in medical school, I did the bulk of my training at a large teaching hospital in San Diego. I was taken aback by the degree of suffering that I saw every day: Wards filled with suffering; both children and adults in pain and dying. Family members were grief stricken. The pain on so many levels was deep, dark and palpable.

I still remember the very first patient I ever took care of. She was a teenage girl who battled a disease in which the pulmonary arteries in her

I was taken aback by the degree of suffering that I saw every day . . .

lungs were chronically blocked by clots. While other kids her age were out enjoying life, she was bed bound and confined to the ICU. Her only hope for survival was a very risky surgery to try and remove the clots. She was such a sweet kid and despite her suffering, she always seemed to try and put on a smile when her friends and family would come visit her. I remember the day of her surgery; I told her she would be fine and that I would see her when she gets out. She just gave me that smile as they wheeled her away. It was the last time I ever saw her. She died on the operating table. Her young life was gone, and her family would forever be scarred with this horrible loss.

Sadly, that was just a microcosm of the world around us. Do you know nearly 10 million people suffer greatly and eventually die every year from cancer? There are 18 million who are stricken with and eventually die from heart disease every year. Infectious disease ravages and kills nearly 17 million every year, many of whom are children. Approximately 3.1 million children die from undernutrition each year (UNICEF, 2018a). Just think about how horrifying that is . . . this means nearly 60,000 children die every week from undernutrition. In addition, there is suffering from crimes, natural disasters and acts of terrorism and wars. If we look at our world honestly for what it is—it is wrecked. Suffering is immense. Let's be brutally honest here. A force that is causing this level of suffering in our world must be evil. There can be no other explanation for what we see.

And that is exactly what the Bible says. In 1 John 5:19 it tells us that: *"the whole world lies in the power of the evil one."* Ephesians 2:2 teaches us that Satan is the: *"prince and the power of the air."* During the temptation of Christ (Matthew 4), Satan reminds Jesus that the kingdoms of the world were his (Satan's) to give. Jesus did not argue the point. Finally, a passage that surprises many people is from Hebrews 2:14 which tells us that Satan is the one who holds *"the power of death."* The Bible is clear on this. Satan yields power. He has the power of death. And when you see the pain and the suffering and the brokenness of the world around us . . . yeah, this makes sense . . . a lot of sense.

A force that is causing this level of suffering in our world must be evil.

Genesis described how this happened. God made our world in perfection. There was to be no pain, no suffering, no heartache and no death. It was made to be paradise. But God warned us that should humankind choose to go the other direction, and choose sin, then paradise would be lost. Satan would then have power. As a result, suffering and death would become the norm. That is exactly what we see in our world today—dark skies.

Thankfully, God's story does not end there. God loves us so much that even though it was humankind who chose sin from the beginning, it was God Who sent His Son to fix the mess that we had created. Through His death on the cross, for those who accept Christ, someday that paradise will be restored forever.

But for now, in this broken world that you and I live, Satan yields very real power, and he is the one who darkens even the bluest skies of our lives. Why does that matter? Because it allows us to direct our anger against the evil that has caused it. It drives us then to cling to the One who can work all things together for good. It drives us to the shelter of Jesus when the Enemy has turned our skies dark.

As a pastor, I understood very clearly who the author was of pain and suffering in this world. This was vital for me to understand when my skies turned dark from this illness. How could I possibly turn to God for His comfort and healing if deep down I believed He was the One doing this to me? There are those who try to cling to those platitudes that sound nice on paper: "*God has a reason. God has a purpose. God is teaching you something. Who can know the mind of God?*" Yeah, that sounds nice and flowery when your skies are blue.

> *...it allows us to direct our anger against the evil that has caused it. ... then to cling to the ... shelter of Jesus ...*

But when you are in a crisis and your world has been ripped inside out, it does not work!

When I feel like throwing up every morning and

How could I possibly turn to God for His comfort and healing if deep down I believed He was the One doing this to me?

struggle to even stand upright, it does not work that *God has a reason.* When the sickness has robbed me of every ounce of energy and I am scared for the future, it brings me no solace that *I can't know the mind of God.* Sure, Pastor Andy, God has a reason for your suffering, you just can't know what it is, but He has a reason. Nope. If God caused such horrible suffering in my life and my family, then that would not be a God I want in my life.

Don't let Satan win twice in your life. Instead, let's direct our anger towards the Enemy—the perpetrator—and turn our trust and faith to Christ. In doing so, we begin to tap into the power of God to transform those dark skies.

But the fact I understood it was Satan that did this to me changed everything. I directed my anger towards him. I vowed to do everything in my limited power to get back at him for what he did to me. And that means turning to my Hero, my Savior, my God for the strength and the power that I would need to deal with those skies the Enemy has darkened.

Sometimes people will ask, "if Satan has very real power and he is the one causing this suffering, then why bother even praying and going to God?" Please understand that there is a big difference between God did not cause your skies to be darkened and God can't do anything about it. Throughout scripture you see God working through a broken world. You see the Enemy constantly darkening the skies of humankind and God fervently fighting on our behalf. Can God fix every problem that the Enemy throws at us and do it instantly and completely? Eventually, yes. But if He did it right now then our current world would be Heaven. But God, even in a broken world, fights for us. Even in a world stained with sin, where Satan is *the ruler of this world*, God still steps in and *works all things together for good*. Are all

You see the Enemy constantly darkening the skies of human-kind and God fervently fighting on our behalf.

things good? No, not in this world. For now, Satan can and does darken our skies. And while those dark skies cannot always be completely taken away, God can and will step into those storms of life and work fervently on our behalf.

I have dealt with this horrible illness now for seventeen years. I understand that things like this not only happen, but are expected in a fallen, broken world where Satan is the *prince and power of the air.* I know that as my Heavenly Father, God will do everything He can for me. What parent would not heal their kid who was suffering if they could. I am a dad myself and if my kids suffer, I can assure you it is even worse for me to watch them go through it. And the fact that my illness continues is a clear reminder that we are not yet in Heaven, and that all the problems in this broken world will not be fixed until we are there. God loves me. I am His kid. God loves you and if you have chosen for Christ then you are His kid also. And when you hurt, He hurts. He is your Dad and would never bring this harm into your life.

I actively (and mentally) fight that tendency that wants to blame God. I actively (and mentally) fight that tendency that wants to blame God. He has been the hero throughout this. He is my strength and my rock. As my Heavenly Father, He has carried me through some of the darkest times in my life. I have not just survived during these dark skies, but at times I have even prevailed. And that has come only by the power of a loving God working through the mess the Enemy has created.

One of the recurring themes that will be developed in this book is that the only answer to life when our skies become dark is God. It is the power of God working in and through a very broken world that can brighten our dark skies. But that all comes to a screeching halt if we buy into the lie of the Enemy that says it is God Who has caused or allowed these dark skies in our life.

And that does bring up the issue of *caused* vs. *allowed*. Some may say that while God does not cause the tragedy, He does *allow* it. And that makes it ok. Really, are we going to be okay with that amid our suffering? How would we view a parent if he or she could stop tragedy from coming upon their child, but they *allowed* it anyway? It is in their power to take suffering away from their child, but they allow it to happen anyway? How would I feel if I knew God can take this disease out of my life, but is choosing to *allow* it to happen? If God can stop it, but does not, then that is cruel. And that is not a God I want in my life.

It is inconsistent with the character of our loving, Heavenly Father that He is the One either causing or even allowing tragedy

> *How would we view a parent if he or she could stop tragedy from coming upon their child, but they allowed it anyway?*

in our life. It is Satan as the temporary "ruler of this world" who is solely responsible.

As we proceed, we are going to start looking at a variety of ways that God miraculously fights on our behalf when our skies are dark. But we will never be able to tap into that kind of power if we continue to hold onto the false assumption that God is the one who either caused or is allowing that suffering. It will only lead to bitterness; bitterness at life and ultimately bitterness toward God.

So, let us not give Satan the double victory by attributing to God what the Enemy has brought into our life. Instead, let's direct our anger towards the Enemy—the perpetrator—and turn our trust and faith to Christ. In doing so, we begin to tap into the power of God to transform those dark skies.

Author's Prayer

Father,
I know You did not bring these dark clouds into my life.
But the enemy did. And God I know You are my Dad, and
this breaks Your heart for me to go through this. I will not
give the enemy a double victory and blame You for what
he has done. Instead, Father I will love You even more and
depend on You even stronger. I know that You will take
me through this. Give me power, strength and Your peace
and wisdom to handle what the enemy has done.
In Jesus' Name, Amen.

Rx PRESCRIPTION FOR WHEN SKIES AREN'T BLUE

Take these important steps this week:

1) Be alert to the tendency that we have to blame God for our suffering.

2) If you are blaming God, immediately recognize it and turn that anger back on the real perpetrator—Satan.

3) Ask God for forgiveness for blaming Him.

4) Then ask God for strength, knowing that your loving Father will guide you through this dark sky time.

Andy Laurie

ANDY LAURIE, MD

When Skies Aren't Blue

PREPARE FOR THE DARK SKIES

On September 4, 1888, George Eastman founded the Kodak corporation. In the 20th century, photography and Kodak were essentially synonymous. Just taking that special picture became known as a "Kodak moment". The Kodak corporation became a member of the Dow Jones, one of the industrial giants in the world. By the 1980s they employed over 140,000 people world-wide and by the early 1990s had a peak revenue of over $16 Billion. And yet on January 19, 2012, this one-time corporate giant, this seemingly invincible force, filed chapter 11 bankruptcy. The greatness that was at one time Eastman Kodak was no more.

What happened? The explanation is a simple, but sad one. They were not prepared when the winds of change blew. There was a major shift in photography away from traditional film and into the digital age. Kodak did not recognize this in time to make the necessary changes and adaptations. They could not compete because they were not prepared, and they were taken by surprise and ended up losing the battle, badly.

What about you and me? When the winds of change blow in our life and our blue skies become dark, are we going to be ready? Will we be prepared? Will we be spiritually strong to fight that battle? Or will it take us by surprise? This is not a trivial point. That is why God went out of His way to make sure you and I would be prepared for the coming of darker skies. It is the battles that we do not see coming that are the most devastating.

In 1 Peter 5:8 God warns us that we are to, "*. . . be alert. Your adversary, the devil, prowls around like a roaring lion seeking someone to devour.*" God is emphatically reminding us that there is a very real Enemy out there whose desire is to destroy our lives and ultimately destroy our souls. This Enemy is constantly darkening our skies and God says be alert, be ready, and do not let it take you by surprise when it does happen. Be prepared to fight the battle.

Jesus alerted us to the battle in John 16:33 with this warning: "*These things I have spoken to you, so that in Me you may have peace. In the world you* **It is the battles that we do not see coming that are the most devastating.** *have tribulation, but take courage; I have overcome the world.*" Jesus told us that we will have tribulation. He told us very clearly that there will be times our skies would be darkened. But we do not need to fear because He has overcome this dark world and is fighting on our behalf. God is telling us that we cannot be taken by surprise. We need to be ready. We need to be prepared.

Why is God telling us this? God is not being the celestial killjoy in the sky. He is not trying to create a bunch of Christian pessimists. He is not trying to get us to be a glass half-empty type people. Quite the opposite. Throughout scripture God challenges us to seek His joy and His peace. God even admonishes us to remember that *"this is the day the Lord has made so let us rejoice and be glad in it."* (Psalm 118:24).

God is telling us to be ready. We need to prepare.

So, why is God warning us about the dangers of this world? This is about God giving us a realistic view on life, so that when (not if) our skies become darkened we are not taken by surprise. Because it is the surprise and the lack of preparation that can make things so much worse.

I think one of the best illustrations of how to view life when our skies are not blue was laid out in James 1:2 which says, *"Consider it pure joy, my brethren, when you face trials of many kinds."* I find it fascinating that God did not say consider it pure joy *if* you face trials of many kinds. But He said *when*. This is a clear statement that it is not if your skies will turn dark, but rather in a broken world it is when they will turn dark.

So, God said we would face trials of *"many kinds"*. The English translation for "many kinds" is "polka dots". Interesting concept! God is telling us that our life will be polka dotted with problems of many kinds. Picture your life as a giant painting canvas. On that canvas, imagine that you have many circles or dots. Some of these dots are green and those represent the good things going on in your life. Some of these dots are red and they represent the problems and the struggles in life.

THE CANVAS OF LIFE

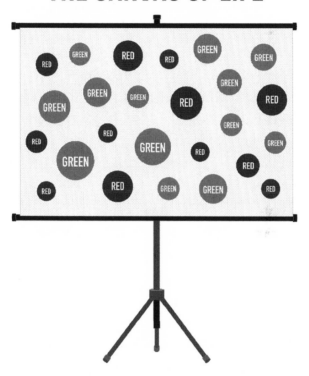

Our life is filled with both green (good) dots and red (bad) dots. That is life. We simultaneously have both the good and the bad going on at the same time. Life is not a situation where it is all good and all wonderful all the time. Then, some tragedy happens, and suddenly it is nothing but all bad and all horrible all the time. That is not life and we know that. As we travel down the road of life, it will constantly be polka dotted with both the good and the bad. And these dots are constantly in flux. Sometimes there are more green dots than red, and the skies seem kind of blue. Sometimes the red dots seem to dominate, and the skies get extra dark. Let's face it, sometimes in life the skies are both blue and dark at the same time. The good and the bad are both going on. That is how life works. That is how God wants us to see life.

There is tremendous power in seeing life this way. We will not be floored every time a red dot comes into our life. We expect it. We do not like it. It is not enjoyable; that is why God said "*consider it pure joy*" because it is not joyful. But we have to think differently about those red dots.

If we understand they are part of life and we even expect it, we can prepare accordingly. We do not have false expectations that life should be nothing but good (green dots). You see if we are operating under false expectations that life should be a certain way and when inevitably it is not, that leads to bitterness. And when the roots of bitterness settle into our life, it turns us away from God, away from others, and leads us into an even darker place. It is a vicious circle. The Enemy throws a red dot into our life and thereby darkens our sky. Because we do not have realistic expectations, bitterness sets in. That bitterness eats away at our relationship with God, which in turn further darkens our skies. We must learn to break that vicious circle.

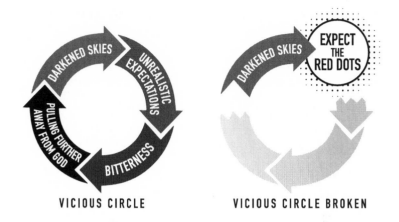

VICIOUS CIRCLE   VICIOUS CIRCLE BROKEN

When I became ill, on so many levels it was devastating. I went from being strong and vibrant to barely hanging on to life. Physically, because of the disease, I felt just horrible at times. And then there were the very scary questions: How would I survive? Who would take care of my family? All that work to become a doctor, would it be for nothing? What would happen to the brand-new church we just started? Talk about major red dots showing up everywhere!

But I will say this, while this was horrible, I was not taken by surprise. I taught on this many times at the church. This is a broken world. Life is polka dotted with the good and the bad. I understood very clearly that in a broken world, red dots, even big, horrible ones like what I was now facing, are a reality. And it is the Enemy, not God, who brought those red dots into my life. It is the Enemy, not God, who darkened those skies. So, while I was rocked from this, I was not surprised. I was devastated, but not bitter.

I was rocked from this. I was not surprised. I was devastated, but not bitter.

So yes, my life now had some major red dots. And while I was not surprised, I was overwhelmed. It is one thing to say that I intellectually understood that life was fragile and can be rocked so easily. But, it can be overwhelming when it becomes reality and those big old red dots smack you to the ground. It is a whole new level of devastation when your skies have been darkened beyond what you think you can cope. What then? What is next?

Author's Prayer

Father,
You told me in this broken world my life would be polka dotted with struggles and problems. Father my skies have turned dark. I am hurting. I don't know how to cope with all of this. I know the Enemy is the cause of this. I will not turn away from You because of this. But I am overwhelmed now God. I need Your power and Your strength. My skies are very dark right now. Help me Father.
In Jesus' Name, Amen

PRESCRIPTION FOR WHEN SKIES AREN'T BLUE

Put these steps into practice once a week:

1) Think about the scriptures from Jesus which caution us of the inevitable troubles that we will face (red dots).

2) Ask God to guide you and strengthen you ahead of time so that you will be prepared for whatever those troubles may be.

3) Think about all the things you have in your life right now that are good (green dots).

4) Thank God for all those green dots, especially given this is a broken world.

Andy Laurie

ANDY LAURIE, MD

When Skies Aren't Blue

TAKE ACTION

I have practiced medicine for nearly three decades. I have seen a trend develop over the recent years. We have encouraged patients to take a more active role in their medical care. We are discovering that the more engaged the patient . . . more often, the better the outcome.

In the last chapter we discussed those red polka dots that darken our skies. They can take the form of a physical health crisis, mental health struggles, broken families, broken marriages, painful relationships, financial distress and so much more. Those red dots are very much part of life in this broken world. But when they hit, it is so important that we do not just accept it passively, but we take some action.

Certainly, when it comes to failing physical health, one of the first steps to taking action is seeking out medical care. They say doctors make the worst patients. That is probably true to a degree. Sometimes as physicians we think we know what is best for ourselves, and we are unwilling to seek that wisdom from others. I have to admit that was me—guilty as charged! As a physician I rarely if ever went to the

When those red dots hit, do not just accept it passively, but take some action.

doctor. I just figured if anything happened to me I would just handle it myself. And that worked . . . until I got sick! When this illness hit, I realized that this illness was beyond my understanding.

I needed help from others who knew more than I. And I did everything within reason that I could do. I saw the appropriate specialists. They attempted various procedures and prescribed different medications. It was very much a trial and error process.

Some of the procedures and medications made things better and others made things worse. Anyone who battles chronic illness understands the ups and downs that go with trying new therapies. And we also understand how incredibly frustrating and at times heart breaking it can be when a new therapy fails to bring relief. I shed many tears during those times when my hopes of a new therapy would be dashed.

But I did follow the advice of the medical experts. In the end, was it a complete cure for me? No. But it did help significantly. I got to the point where I could begin to eat and drink small portions again without continuously vomiting. I got to the point where I was able to stay upright for at least limited period of times without losing consciousness.

These were huge steps for me. But, did it take away all the suffering? No. This is a chronic disease, and it will be a continuous struggle for me. But it did get me to the point where I could at least have some semblance of a life again. Without the guidance from the medical experts, I would not have survived. Taking that action and seeking out medical care was to say the least vitally important.

As important as it is to seek out medical care if we are suffering from physical health problems, it is equally important when we are dealing with psychological and emotional problems. If someone is suffering from a psychological battle such as depression/anxiety and others, my first advice as "Pastor Andy" is to go see a physician.

The reality is many psychological conditions are not spiritual problems. Someone can be rock-solid with God and still suffer greatly from depression, anxiety and other emotional and psychiatric conditions. Often the problem is not spiritual. As a pastor over the years, people have come to me requesting spiritual counseling for issues related to depression and anxiety and other psychological issues. I almost universally start with telling them to first go see their doctor and then afterwards come back and talk with me. The majority of the time they end up seeing their doctor and the problem is treated with success. And that is because the problem is ultimately a chemical imbalance that needs correcting rather than a spiritual issue. So, step one when

Without the guidance from the medical experts, I would not have survived.

dealing with health problems (physical or psychological) is to take some action and start by seeing a doctor. Many times, the answer is found there, and healing can begin.

While this is a book dealing with health issues, certainly the principle of acting would apply to any area of life that is darkening our skies. Some may say that this is bypassing God, leaving Him out of the equation. Not at all. God often brings healing through the actions that we take. God even tells us in Proverbs 16:9 that, *"the mind of man plans his way. But the Lord directs his steps."* If we are right with God, then we can have the confidence to know that God will work through the actions that we take. I have seen God do that many times in my life and even through this devastating illness. Initiate what you need to do and take action. God often brings a level of healing or resolution through those very actions.

It is awesome to watch God work through our actions and bring that healing and brighten those dark skies. And when that happens, we are so grateful to God. But let's be honest. It does not always play out that way.

God often brings healing through the actions that we take.

This brings us to perhaps the most difficult part of our skies turning dark. And that is the painful reality that despite our action, those skies may remain dark. The problem is not going away. The hurt remains. Despite all our efforts this dark sky is not turning blue. It is seemingly an unchangeable problem. What then?

Author's Prayer

Father,

These dark skies will not go away. I have done all I can do.
Thank you that there has been some improvement. But I
am still suffering, and I am frustrated and I am scared.
What should I do? Where should I turn? I am hanging on
the best I can. But I just don't know how much longer
I can do this. Help, please help.
In Jesus' Name, Amen.

PRESCRIPTION FOR
WHEN SKIES AREN'T BLUE

Take these important steps this week:

1) Remember that God often works through the actions that we take. (Proverbs 16:9)

2) Don't passively accept your dark sky and do nothing about it.

3) Depending on your specific struggle—take appropriate action to deal with it. Seek out the help of a physician, trusted friend, caring family member, a psychologist/ counselor, a pastor, etc.

Andy Laurie

ANDY LAURIE, MD

When Skies Aren't Blue

LET THE OLD LIFE GO

The first few years of my illness were a whirlwind of medical activity. It was appointment after appointment, test after test, procedures and surgeries. I went to all the specialists, and I did everything that I could possibly do to find healing. There were no more medical options available. There was nothing else to be done.

While there was some degree of improvement, there was no cure. This was going to be my life. It was a far cry from the vibrant, healthy man I used to be. Every morning I wake up with what feels like the flu and wonder how severe it will be that day. Simple joys like eating are now a struggle. The battle with nausea and abdominal pain is on-going. It is a fight just to keep enough calories to sustain myself. I used to have boundless energy, juggling two careers and a big family. Now there are many times that I can barely stand upright. Heart arrythmias are now commonplace. Simple tasks that I never even gave a thought about are now overwhelming and draining. I am dependent on medication to function at even the most basic of level just to stay alive. Everything is now just hard. The skies had turned very dark and it was not going to change. This was my life.

Coming to grips with my reality was incredibly difficult, and early into the disease I had sunk into a deep depression. I would lay in bed for weeks on end, all the lights off, the blinds closed and stare up into the nothingness of the ceiling. It felt like I was in a dark tunnel. But this one seemingly had no light at the end of it. No blue skies. Nothing but darkness.

It was not just feeling physically lousy from the illness that sent me to this dark place. It was also the lamenting of the loss of the life I used to have. It was the realization that I was going to be sick every day for the rest of my life. It was knowing that I would never be able to do those things that I used to be able to do. And it was that realization—more than anything—which sent me to that very dark place. It was a horrible place without hope that I never want to go to again, ever.

> *It felt like I was in a dark tunnel. . . . that had no light at the end of it.*

How does one cope with that level of darkness? How can one have joy and hope again? Where can it be found? How can one break free from those dark chains?

I don't often quote Dumbledore from Harry Potter, but he said something that is so profound to this very situation: *"Happiness can be found, even in the darkest of times, if one only remembers to turn on the light."*

Just turn on the light. Seems so easy. But the challenge is to somehow find that switch in depths of the darkness. It's tough, really tough. I had been a pastor for many years. I had counseled people who were in that dark place in their lives on how to turn that switch on. I knew how to do this. But here is the problem. When we find ourselves rocked by life and our skies have turned dark, we simply do not think well. Everything becomes clouded.

> *But the challenge is to somehow find that switch in depths of the darkness.*

It does not matter whether our dark skies are caused by health issues, broken relationships, tragic loss of loved ones, financial calamity and so on. When those things turn our lives upside down and the darkness overtakes us, we simply do not process life well. We do not think well.

I knew all this stuff. I knew all these principles that I am writing in this book. But amid the darkness, I could not see it. I could not break out of it. I needed someone to show me the way to turn that light back on.

It was a close friend who is also the founding pastor of The Bridge Christian Church, David McAllister, who guided me to find that switch. I cannot stress enough how important it is that you seek out those close to you as you deal with those dark sky times. Our natural tendency is to pull away. The depression draws us towards isolation which leads to further darkness. That is where the Enemy wants you to be—alone. Resist that! The Enemy knows there is great power when you surround yourself with others who will guide you and keep you focused on Christ during those dark sky moments. Seek those people out as you deal with the darkness. You will need it. I did. Proverbs 27:6 tells us that *faithful are the wounds of a friend.* What he said to me hurt. But coming out of the darkness into blue sky is rarely without pain.

I remember so clearly his words. He reminded me of how much he loved me and how much his heart broke for what I have been through. He told me that while I should continue to seek out medical care and look for potential future cures, for now, I have done all that I can do. And modern medicine cannot cure me. This now is my life.

> *The depression draws us towards isolation . . . That is where the Enemy wants you to be—alone. Resist that!*

He reminded me of how many times I have taught from Psalm 118:24: *"This is the day the Lord has made so let us rejoice and be glad in it."* God has given us this day, and only this day. So, for better or worse it is the day that we have and let's make the most of it. He reminded me of Ephesians 5:15-16: *"Be careful how you live . . . be wise . . . make the most of your time."* I will wake up each morning, and I will be sick. That is expected. That is my life.

I cannot lament over what I no longer can do, but rather I need to take joy in what I can do. Will I be sick— yes! Will the nausea be miserable—yes! Will I be so weak

Coming out of the darkness into blue sky is rarely without pain.

and light-headed that I cannot stand at times—yes! It will be all that and more. But that is my life. It is expected. So, I accept it and do what I can do.

Amid an unchanging chronic illness our skies will never turn blue if the specter of our old life keeps us from living our new life. The legendary UCLA coach John Wooden said, *"do not let what you cannot do interfere with what you can do."*

My friend and mentor, Pastor David McAllister, also reminded me that it was Satan who did this to me. And if I ever want to pay the Enemy back for what he did, I better stop lamenting the past and what I cannot do. Instead, I need to start living for God today and watch what He can do in my new life—my new sick life.

He said many other things to me. But the message was clear. It was time to let go of the past and accept the new life. The healthy Andy was gone. He was not coming back. This is the new life.

I listened to all that he had to say. And when he was done, I went into my room, closed the door and in my solace let all that I heard sink in. It is hard to fully put

Our skies will never turn blue if the specter of our old life keeps us from living our new life.

to words what happened next. Here is the best way I can describe it. When I was a kid I would go to the beach, and I remember being hit by one of those big waves. I was just a child, so these waves would just toss me around like a rag doll. They would pull me under the water and roll me around. I was powerless against the sheer force of the flood. I am not a crying type of man. But, oh how I cried. In fact, I wailed. I wailed for the life that would never be there again. I wailed for every healthy sunrise that would be no longer. I wailed for every good meal I would never enjoy again. I wailed for the dad who could no longer keep up with his kids. I wailed for the hopes and dreams that I had as a pastor and a physician that were gone. I wailed for that wonderful life that this disease took.

And then in the same way the wave that took me under as a kid finally released me—I emerged. Tired and worn out, but I emerged. And that switch had been flipped on. The old healthy Andy was gone. The grieving over the past was over. The new Andy was ready for his new life.

Author's Prayer

Father,
I cannot move forward if I keep lamenting the past. As
much as I hate being sick, I cannot break the grips of these
dark skies until I move on. So, Father help me let it go
and embrace my new life with You. Even sick, You tell me
I can still have victory. God, tomorrow is Your new day
that You will give me. Please help me with Your power
and Your peace to truly make the most of it.
In Jesus' Name, Amen.

℞ PRESCRIPTION FOR WHEN SKIES AREN'T BLUE

Take these important steps this week:

1) Decide that you will no longer allow what you can't do interfere with what you can do.

2) You will need to go through the painful process of flipping on that switch and letting that old life go.

3) Do not go through this process alone. Seek out the help of a trusted friend, caring family member, a counselor, a pastor, etc.

Andy Laurie

ANDY LAURIE, MD

When Skies Aren't Blue

REDEFINE VICTORY OVER TODAY

By letting go of the unchangeable of the old life, you have taken a major step forward. You are now ready to have victory over the day. To do that, you must first redefine victory.

To redefine victory, you must first change the way you think. And this begins first thing in the morning. Every morning when I wake up, I go right to the sink to brush my teeth and get my day started. I look at the mirror and see the face of a suffering man who like every morning pretty much feels like garbage. But instead of letting that emotionally pull me down, I put a reminder note taped right next to the mirror. It reads: *Andy, you will feel like garbage when you wake up. You will feel crummy at times throughout the day. You will be limited. This is your life. Don't let what you can't do stop you from doing what you can do. Find victory over the day. Psalm 118:24.*

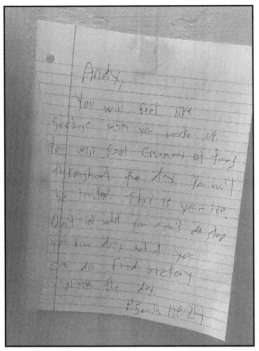

Reminder note from Psalm 118:24—in my doctor handwriting

Did that take away the physical sickness. No. But, instead of lamenting and being depressed over how I feel and what I cannot do, it reminds me to accept my current "sick" life and focus on what I can accomplish. This is my life. Now, Andy, what is your victory going to be?

To help me answer this question I memorized Psalm 118:24: *"This is the day the Lord has made. Let us rejoice and be glad in it."* Okay Andy, you are sick—that is to be expected. But God has given you this day, so find victory in it.

But how can we find victory when we feel so lousy? How can we have victory when our health is going to limit us? The answer is: we redefine victory.

The old Andy would work twelve hours a day between the church and practicing radiology. But the new Andy might only be able to be somewhat productive a few hours here or

But how can we find victory when we feel so lousy? The answer is: we redefine victory.

there at best. Yet, that would be a victory. The old Andy would get out and play sports with his kids. But the new Andy at best could only watch his kids play. But that is a victory. Sometimes it was just getting up, taking a shower and picking up a few items at the grocery store—a victory. Just mustering up the strength to take a short walk and spend that time talking to God in prayer—victory. Taking the time to be able to read the Bible—victory. I used to run an entire church as the pastor, including preparing for and delivering the weekly teaching. That was no longer possible. But now just getting up and making it to church and ministering to even a few people—victory!

What is the victory that you can find today? Take some time and really think through this and come up with a list of things that you can do—things that would be a victory for you. Do not worry about what you cannot do; remember that is the old life. That life is gone and cannot be changed—just focus on what you can do. It does not matter how simple it may be. It does not have to be some earth-shattering accomplishment. It can even be something

What is the victory that you can find today? It does not matter how simple it may be.

that would be fun or enjoyable, a hobby. Just do something. The very fact that it was a struggle for you makes it that much more meaningful. It makes the victory all the sweeter . . . even more heroic.

If we do not do this, we end up entering a downward decline, which makes our underlying health conditions even worse. Here is what happens. Instead of finding something that we can do, we sit around lamenting and mourning over what we cannot do. Guess what that leads to? It brings depression and anxiety. Medically we know how damaging this can be. I can assure you this depression and anxiety will exacerbate whatever illness that you already struggle with. God created us to *do*. We simply do not do well physically, emotionally, psychologically, or spiritually when we are not *doing*.

> *The very fact that it was a struggle for you makes the victory even more heroic.*

Every time those negative thoughts creep back into your head (and it will happen)—that you used to be able to achieve and accomplish so much more—shut them down completely! Those thoughts are poison. Those thoughts will darken your skies. Those thoughts will turn the victory into defeat. Those thoughts are from the Enemy who wants you to lament the past.

It is the Enemy who wants you to live under the dark skies of what you cannot do. God wants you to find joy and victory in the day that He gave you. Be a hero and do it.

I cannot stress enough that we are talking about having victory over just the current day. It is one of the evil tricks of the Enemy to try and get those of us who struggle with chronic illness to worry beyond the day. When we struggle with health issues, just thinking about handling life beyond the day can feel flat out overwhelming. Do not go there. Just focus on finding victory today.

If you recall in the sermon on the mount Jesus reminded us: *"So do not worry about tomorrow; for tomorrow will worry about itself. Each day has enough trouble of its own."* (Matt. 6:34). Great advice

It is the Enemy who wants you to live under the dark skies of what you cannot do.

from our Creator. Just keep your focus on today and today only. Do not allow your mind to drift to the concerns of tomorrow. That will lead to poisonous worry. Victory is just for the day.

Choosing to live our life this way can even bring a sense of fulfillment that we cannot achieve while healthy. When we are healthy, often we come to the end of the day and think about all the things left undone. And that leads to lack of contentment. But I can tell you, for me, I can now truly take pride in whatever things I was able to accomplish for the day. No matter how simple these things may seem, the very fact that I did them while feeling so crummy

Do not worry about tomorrow.

is a big deal. It is the same for you. You can go to bed with the contentment and peace knowing that you did it; you accomplished, you achieved, you are a hero, you made the most out of the day that God gave you.

Another wonderful benefit to approaching life this way is that we no longer take things for granted. We used to do things so easily that we never even gave it a second thought. Now we can take the time and really appreciate and be thankful for even the simplest things in life. Contentment is not an elusive hope, but it will happen by choosing to have victory over the day by doing . . . just by doing.

As you choose to live your life this way, you will notice something. It does not happen right away. It takes time. It is a process.

Contentment will happen by choosing to have victory over the day by doing.

But one incredible day you will look up and notice the sky does not look quite so dark anymore. In fact, it has some shades of blue.

Author's Prayer

Father,

Thank You for giving me this day. I know it is not going to be an easy one, they rarely are anymore. But with Your help Father I will do what I can do and not be brought down by that which I cannot. And in doing so, I will have victory over this day and truly rejoice and be glad in it.

In Jesus' Name, Amen.

℞ PRESCRIPTION FOR WHEN SKIES AREN'T BLUE

Put these steps into action every day during difficult times:

1) Remember, you were created to do—find a victory that you can accomplish today.

2) Remind yourself that even the "small" accomplishments for you are heroic.

3) Leave a reminder note that you will be limited—but you can still have victory.

4) Do not worry about tomorrow—just do it today.

Andy Laurie

ANDY LAURIE, MD

When Skies Aren't Blue

WATCH GOD LIGHT IT UP IN UNEXPECTED WAYS

We have heard the adage that *the Lord works in mysterious ways*. That is not in the Bible; but live a little bit of life and we all can attest to its truth. God is not limited as we are and works on a whole different level. God Himself told us as much: *"For My thoughts are not your thoughts, Nor are your ways My ways, declares the LORD. For as the heavens are higher than the earth, So are My ways higher than your ways And My thoughts than your thoughts."* (Isaiah 55:8-9).

God really does step into our dark sky times and light up those skies in the most unexpected ways. He does things in ways that we could have never seen coming.

But let's face it. We want Him to handle things our way. Usually, that means going to God and insisting that He just takes this struggle (whatever it may be) completely out of our lives. And amazingly enough-often times that is exactly what happens! In fact, if you look back on your life, no doubt there were issues and struggles that were so concerning for you at the time. Yet now, you barely remember them. Maybe it was a health issue, a relationship issue or a financial problem that was all-consuming at the time and now it is just a distant memory.

God deals with those things for us all the time. We should be incredibly grateful and not forget all those times that He came through and did in fact just take those problems away. I really do encourage you to take some time and list out all the things over the past decade or two that were such a problem and now realize they are just gone—a bad memory that has long been forgotten. God deserves the credit for doing this. But what happens when it does not play out this way? What do we do when those struggles are not totally taken away?

We want God to just take this struggle completely out of our life.

As we discussed earlier, we live in a broken and fallen world; and we are essentially on Enemy territory. Satan yields tremendous power and as scripture tells us *"the whole world lies in the power of the evil one"* (1 John 5:19). So, the reality we must accept is there will be those times that we will have struggles. There will be dark sky times. We are not in heaven yet. In this world, we will have those issues that are seemingly unchangeable. If we do not grasp this, it will lead to tremendous frustration in life and ultimately with God.

This reality hit me about two years into my illness. I remember it so clearly. It was one of those God moments you just do not forget. I was praying, and as was my practice, I was pleading with God to take this illness from me. I had been doing this for two years. But this

What do we do when those struggles are not totally taken away?

day was to be different. God was about to open my eyes and give me a glimpse of how He sees things.

One of my kids was going through a difficult situation in their life. I was thinking about the situation as I was praying to God. It broke my heart to see my kid suffer. And then it hit me. God is my Dad. God is the perfect Father in every way. And we are created in His Image. If I feel that way about my kids, how much more so does God feel that way towards me, His kid. It broke my heart to realize how much my

God was about to open my eyes . . .

suffering hurt Him. He was saying, *My child if you only knew the pain that your illness causes Me and how much it crushes Me to see all the suffering in this broken world.*

I wept hard. I wept not for myself, but for my Dad who had to endure the suffering of His kid. I was reminded of Jesus when He saw the heart break of people who were grieving the death of Lazarus—and scripture tells us that our God *wept.* Indeed, God feels the heart break of His suffering kids more than we can possibly imagine.

From that moment on my prayers to God changed. I pray to Him about how sorry I am that this suffering breaks His heart. I talk to Him about how painful it must be for Him, as a parent, to endure this. Instead of desper-

From that moment on my prayers to God have changed. ate pleading to totally take away all my suffering, I focused instead on the fact that my loving Father is still right there with me. I spend time thanking Him as an awesome Dad. He is blessing me even in the middle of these dark skies.

When our prayers are nothing but a desperate plea to God, we end up blinding ourselves to the truly amazing things that He is in fact doing. That is exactly what happened to me. And when I finally recognized this, my eyes were opened to the ways that God was working behind the scenes during this health disaster the Enemy threw on me. I began to clearly see how God was taking care of me amid the darkness of this lousy disease. I began to see how He was lighting up the dark skies in most unexpected ways.

Take my health for example. When the disease hit, I was at the point that I did not think I would even survive. And even though this was not a well recognized disease at the time, God guided me to the right people who were able to make a diagnosis and help. While the treatment ultimately was not a cure (as I still do suffer from this disease), it brought me to a point where I could at least eat and drink once again. I could at least again stand upright and walk. I could at least have some semblance of a life. Through these wonderful treatments, God was able to get me back to a position where I could at least work part time again as a physician and a pastor. It was truly an answered prayer. I was again able to spend quality time with my wife and my kids and be a husband and a father . . . again wonderful and amazing. Never again will I take such things for granted. And countless times over the years God has stepped in and brought healing throughout this disease.

Let me share with you something that happened a few years back. My heart spontaneously went into an abnormal rhythm called atrial fibrillation. This happens periodically with me due to the dysautonomia disease and the imbalance of how my heart is regulated. But this time it was prolonged, and I went into the hospital as it was getting hard to stay conscious.

Countless times over the years God has stepped in and brought healing throughout this disease.

They admitted me and put me on telemetry to monitor my heart. The cardiologist consulted and decided that if I do not convert back to my normal rhythm by the next morning that he would need to cardiovert me. Yes, that is where they put the shock paddles to your chest and shock you back to normal rhythm. Needless to say, that has very real risks and was not something I was looking forward to.

My wife and I start praying, asking God to heal the atrial fibrillation and if possible do it in such a way that He gets all the credit. If not, then please keep me safe through the procedure and help it to be successful.

Well, the night passed, and the morning came and unfortunately, I was still in the atrial fibrillation rhythm. The cardiologist and his team were coming into the room to set up for the cardioversion procedure. It was Sunday morning, and it was about the time that our church was having services. As they were getting the room prepared for the procedure, we told the nurse who was setting things up that our church would be praying shortly, so we will see what happens. They continued to roll all the equipment in including the defibrillation machine. I was getting quite anxious looking at those shock paddles. As they were getting ready to "hook me up", one of them said, *"wait, stop, look at the monitor; he is back in normal rhythm again!"*

A flood of relief came over me. I asked them to please look at the telemetry strip and tell me the precise time that I converted back to normal rhythm, and they said it was 9:46 AM. My wife and I got this big smile. This would be just after the time in the service that the church would be praying.

The medical team taking care of me called it the "miraculous cardioversion".

God made it clear that this one was from Him. It is kind of funny, but when I followed up the next week with my cardiologist, he told me that the medical team taking care of me at the hospital started calling what happened the "miraculous cardioversion."

When I got home from the hospital, I placed a small note in my room and it simply read 9:46. Every time I pass by, I am reminded how God is actively working through this illness. Over the years, God has done this time and time again. I have faced innumerable health challenges. Each time they all felt overwhelming and yet, *somehow*, I managed to not only get through it, but often prevailed.

I have been brought back from the edge so many times over the years. There is no other explanation other than God letting me know that even in this broken world, He is still right there with

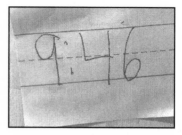

Reminder note in my room

me. And knowing that gives me the confidence that one way or another God will take me through this illness . . . He always has, and He always will.

It is not just with my health where He has done this. He has provided for our financial needs in ways that are flat-out astonishing. When this disease hit, I was distraught with the reality that I had no way to provide for my family. I had a wife and

God has brought me back from the edge so many times over the years.

four young kids. I was too sick to practice medicine at the time. How would we survive? As a man needing to provide for his family, this concern was all-consuming. But I remembered the words of Jesus: *"Do not worry then, saying, 'What will we eat?' or 'What will we drink?' or 'What will we wear for clothing?' For the Gentiles eagerly seek all these things; for your heavenly Father knows that you need all these things. But seek first His kingdom and His righteousness, and all these things will be added to you."* (Matthew 6:33).

God promised as I put Him first and trust in Him, He has got this. *Do not worry Andy. You have enough to deal with in this illness. I have got this one.* And wow did He!

As it turned out, many years back, when I was young and healthy in my medical residency training, my wife and I decided to take a disability insurance policy. They were offering some special policies to young doctors in training at more affordable rates that could be enacted in the future should it ever be needed. We were young, and we did not have much extra income. We never dreamed we would ever need such a policy as we had no health issues. Yet, *for some reason,* we acted on it and took the policy. We had no idea at the time what would have prompted us to do such a thing. But looking back now it is clear that God was protecting us for the future. You see, it was that extra disability insurance that allowed us to keep our house, pay the bills and keep food on the table. It is astonishing what God does if we only open our eyes enough to see Him at work. He is working on our problems long before we even know there is a problem.

It is astonishing what God does if we only open our eyes enough to see Him at work.

With respect to my medical career, it was devastating to me to think that I could not practice being a physician any longer after only a relatively short time in the field. I put in thirteen years of training after high school to get my degree and the thought that it was potentially over was crushing me. But I knew with my health problems, I could not possibly head into the hospital each day and work those long shifts.

My heavenly Father knew exactly what I needed and

once again, He came through. As it *"just so happened"*, my radiology group was willing to work out a situation where I could work from home. Technology *"just so happened"* to progress to a point where they could take the images in the hospital and then send it to my home computer. I could work from home exactly as if I were in the hospital. And on top of that the radiology group was amazing in their flexibility allowing me to work those hours only when I felt well enough to do so. I could not draw up a better scenario in which someone with this devastating illness could still practice on a part-time basis a career that he loves. I was able to do this for many satisfying years.

Eventually, the disease progressed to the point that I could no longer practice. But I still had a full and wonderful career of many years—no regrets at all. Looking back at all the things that needed to be put into place for this to *just so happen* can only be explained by the hand of God taking care of His kid. As I mentioned earlier, God is the God of it *"just so happened"*.

God also knew that my dream of starting a church, being a pastor, and making that difference for Him was seemingly ended because of my health. As I mentioned earlier, I had just gotten the new east side campus of The Bridge Christian Church up and running when this illness hit. I was the only pastor of the church and was the one responsible for all aspects of

God is the God of *"it just so happened."*

that location, including the weekly teaching. There was no way I could continue that with my failing health.

It looked like my dream was going to come crashing down. But then something seemingly miraculous happened. The church from which we branched off suggested that we "pipe in" the teaching from their campus using a live simulcast. However, our campus was roughly twenty miles across the city and there was no easy way to do that at the time. This was before the day of high-speed internet and video conferencing which is so accessible and seamless now. There were some major hurdles to being able to pull this off. While it is now routine for many of the larger churches to simulcast their teaching to multiple satellite churches, it was not then. We would have to become pioneers if this church were to survive. And that we were. We worked through the limited technology that was available and managed to pull it off. There were lots of hurdles and setbacks along the way. But we did it. We were one of the first live feed churches in the entire nation.

It looked like my dream was going to come crashing down.

The church flourished. I was able to focus what strength I had on doing what I genuinely wanted to do, and that is ministering to people. All those other pastoring responsibilities that would have been overwhelming for me because of my health were remedied by the linking of the churches through the technology. The church grew. In fact, we grew right out of our building and into a much larger campus. People were coming and getting right with God, and yeah, I got to be their pastor! Even as sick as I was, I got to make that difference for Christ. How awesome is that! I have no doubt God could have easily just replaced me, and the church would have been fine. But I would not have been fine. It would have crushed my dream to step down. So, He stepped in. And in this incredible way allowed me to continue the dream that had finally begun of being a pastor for The Bridge Christian Church.

I would also say I am a better pastor because of this illness. I can help people in ways that I could never have done if I were healthy. I can relate to others going through difficult times in a very real way and show them how God can work powerfully in their lives in those dark sky moments. In a broken world, that can be so comforting. Scripture tells us: *"Blessed be the God and Father of our Lord Jesus Christ, the Father of mercies and God of all comfort, who comforts us in all our affliction so that we will be able to comfort those who are in any affliction with the comfort with which we ourselves are comforted by God."* (2 Corinthians 1:3-4). God brings us comfort and healing on so many levels. We can then turn right around and share that with others who are suffering.

God also has worked through this illness in a remarkable way to bring me a sense of joy in my family that I really do believe otherwise would not have happened. Prior to my illness, I was burning the candle at both ends. I was working full-time as a doctor to pay the bills. Also, I was putting near full-time hours without taking salary as a pastor in running the new church. That was unsustainable, and I am certain it would have taken a toll on my family. How could I possibly have the time to invest in my wife and kids while trying to juggle these massive responsibilities? This illness forced me to slow down. I simply had no choice any longer.

Earlier in the book, I talked about redefining "victory". I had to simplify and find victory in those things I could do and not those big career items that I could no longer do. And that is the gift of God indeed working in mysterious but wonderful ways. I learned to take joy and victory in some really special, albeit simple things. Sometimes it was just watching my kids play sports, or it was being their coach when my health permitted, maybe it was taking family vacations when I felt up to it, or it was just spending quiet time hanging out with my wife.

My kids are nearly grown now and on their own. Much of the parenting years have now passed, and my wife and I are moving into the "empty nest" phase of life. But while the nest may be almost empty, I have a treasure chest full of wonderful memories, more valuable than any career could have brought.

Despite being sick, I am a very content man. Satan figured he would destroy my life, my hopes, and my dreams with this illness. Satan figured that seventeen years ago when he darkened my skies with sickness that he had me. But he underestimated my Heavenly Father who looked right back at him, and if I may paraphrase scripture a bit, said to the evil one: *you meant evil against my kid, but I used it for good . . .*

And that is the gift of God working in mysterious but wonderful ways.

(Genesis 50:20). God has worked through this illness in ways I could never have fathomed and has brought me a full and rich life.

And this is exactly what God does in the lives of all His kids. Whatever is darkening the skies in your life, do know that God is working hard behind the scenes on your behalf. It breaks His heart that His kids suffer in this broken world. But He will, in incredible ways, walk us through even the darkest situations. Our job is to put our trust and faith in Him and put Him first (Proverbs 3:5, 6). If we do that, we can have the confidence to know that our Heavenly Father will work in mysterious but wonderful ways to brighten even the darkest of skies.

Author's Prayer

Father,
I know that as my Dad seeing me suffer breaks Your heart.
I am so sorry that You are having to go through this too.
But You are an amazing Father, and I have seen You work
through this illness in truly miraculous ways. I know You
always have and always will be right there fighting for
me. The Enemy set out to darken my skies through this
illness and yet what he meant for evil, You transformed it
in ways I could never even have dreamed. Thank You for
being an amazing Dad. I love You.
In Jesus' Name, Amen.

℞ PRESCRIPTION FOR WHEN SKIES AREN'T BLUE

Take these important steps this week:

1) Focus on the reality that your suffering also breaks the heart of your loving Heavenly Father. Grieve with Him.

2) Ask your Father to take you through this awful struggle that the Enemy has caused.

3) Then watch for and fully anticipate God to light up your skies in those most unexpected ways.

Andy Laurie

ANDY LAURIE, MD

When Skies Aren't Blue

BATTLE THAT GOD AMNESIA

It is amazing how God steps in and brightens even the darkest of skies. But it is astounding how often we end up forgetting what He has done. There is just something about the human condition—we tend to develop this God amnesia syndrome.

Here is what happens to many Christians. We face a difficult situation. In fact, it can feel flat out overwhelming. We totally freak out. We do not know how we are going to handle it. This brings tremendous stress and worry into our life. We then cry out to God for help. God steps in and in His amazing ways deals with the problem for us. We are so thankful at the time for what He has done.

But then, some time passes, and we forget the crisis including all that God did to step in and deal with it. Then guess what? Because this world is a mess and full of struggles, we end up facing a similar problem in the future. Of course, we once again totally freak out. We do not know how we are going to handle it and we again are over-

whelmed with stress and worry. It is the cycle of worry!
How powerful would it be if we could simply remember
that God has brought us through a similar situation in the
past and because of that we can have total confidence that
He will carry us through it once again.

I cannot tell you how critical this has been for me in
dealing with this illness. Often, because of the nature of
this autonomic disease, I find myself facing a recurrent
health crises. Perhaps the circumstances are somewhat different, or the symptoms may be slightly changed, but the
bottom line is that the overall theme is the same. And that
is these situations feel overwhelming, and I often do not

know how I am going to handle it. Yet, each time these crises come my way, I need to remind myself of how in the past God has carried me through it.

We develop this God amnesia syndrome.

So, rather than following my gut reaction which is to panic and worry each time; I can very calmly take it to God, knowing as always—He has got this one! Remembering what God has done for us in the past is the key to keeping peace and confidence during future storms of life.

But—we must remember! We must combat that God amnesia that we all suffer from. Otherwise, we are destined to relive the panic and stress cycle each time these storms come our way. The philosopher George Santayana wrote "Those who cannot remember the past are condemned to repeat it" (*The Life of Reason: Reason in Common Sense.* Scribner's, 1905: 284). Nothing can be truer when applied to our spiritual life. If we fail to remember the amazing things God has done in brightening our dark skies, then the Enemy throws another struggle our way and we will condemn ourselves once again to that pattern of panic and worry.

How do we deal with that? How can we battle that God amnesia? God gives us the answer in scripture. He wants us to build our own pile of rocks! What? Yes, build our own pile of rocks.

Remembering what God has done for us in the past is the key to keeping peace and confidence during future storms of life.

If you look at the book of Joshua, you will see that God stepped in multiple times in miraculous ways as He was leading His people to reclaim their promised land. If you recall, one of the earlier miracles was that God parted the waters of the Jordan River so that His people could safely cross into the promised land. Quite impressive. Following that, God instructed Joshua to set up a memorial consisting of a pile of stones taken from the riverbed. The idea behind that was every time someone passed by and saw the pile of stones it would be a reminder of what God had done. Isn't that fascinating! The God who created us and knows us inside and out understands that our brains at times suffer from this God amnesia. As a result, He tells us that we need to create these reminders of the things that He does for us. If we do not, we rob ourselves of something incredibly powerful.

If we forget, we will condemn ourselves to that pattern of panic and worry.

Like Joshua, we need to be setting up our own pile of rocks—our own reminders of the amazing things God does for us. I can tell you personally that this is even more critical when we are dealing with chronic illness. Here is why. When dealing with illness, we tend to get locked into our own myopic world of sickness. Sometimes we get so focused on the disease and how we are feeling that we fail to step back and see the big picture. Dealing with chronic illness can sometimes even cloud our thinking to a point where we are not rationally making the best choices any longer.

This is kind of a side point, but it is important to avoid making any significant decisions when you are dealing with crises of health. We are not thinking well during these times. But one of the things that causes us to think so poorly during those health crises is God amnesia.

So, God tells us that a key weapon in fighting spiritual amnesia is our own pile of rocks. But how do we practically do

God wants us to build our own pile of rocks.

that? Leaving piles of stones all over your living room is probably not the best idea. But there are ways we can easily remind ourselves of how God has come through. I already mentioned to you in the last chapter that I put a little reminder note in my house that simply reads 9:46. I have it in a place where I see it every day. It reminds me of the time that God healed my fibrillating heart. Each time I walk by it, it reminds me of how God is watching out for me. So, guess what? When I face a new twist in this illness, I do not have to start all over with God. I am instantly reminded that God has come through in the past, and I know He will in the future. There is no need to panic. No need to worry. No need to freak out. God's got this.

Whenever God comes through for you in any area, find a way to record it so you will remember. Maybe have something on your phone, your

We tend to get locked into our own myopic world of sickness.

tablet or computer. You can be old school and just keep a written God diary of all the times God has come through.

I do not know what works best for you. We are all different and we all have our unique ways to remind ourselves of things that are important. But what can be more important than reminding yourself of the incredible ways God is working in your life? *It is a powerful reminder that God's got this.* So, whatever way works best for you, just do it. It takes some time to do this, but it will be well worth it. Start keeping those pile of rocks in your life. You will be amazed at the power, peace, and confidence that this will bring you even during the darkest skies.

Author's Prayer

Father,
It humbles me as I look back on my life and see all the
times that You continue to come through for me. Father,
I know in this broken world the Enemy will continue
to throw garbage my way. But rather than immediately
panic, I will remember my own pile of rocks and take
comfort in You. Because of that, I truly can have that
peace that transcends all understanding; even in what
seems to be the darkest of skies.
In Jesus' Name, Amen.

PRESCRIPTION FOR WHEN SKIES AREN'T BLUE

Put these steps into practice right away:

1) Decide on the best way to keep your own pile of rocks (phone, computer/tablet, written diary etc.).

2) Stay committed to this and each time that God comes through for you—document it.

3) Whenever you face a crisis, immediately review your pile of rocks and draw confidence knowing that God took you through something similar in the past and He will do it again.

Andy Laurie

ANDY LAURIE, MD

When Skies Aren't Blue

DWELL ON THE GREEN DOTS

You can almost imagine the rattling of chains as he wrote the words. The Apostle Paul found himself imprisoned in Rome for doing nothing more than preaching the Gospel of Jesus Christ. He knew full well that his time was limited, and that he was likely going to be executed for his faith. It was going to be brutal. No doubt the fear and the concerns were all there. His freedom as he once knew it was gone. His skies were about as dark as they could get when he wrote these very words: *"Rejoice in the Lord always; again I will say, rejoice! Let your gentle spirit be known to all men. The Lord is near. Be anxious for nothing, but in everything by prayer and supplication with thanksgiving let your requests be made known to God. And the peace of God, which surpasses all comprehension, will guard your hearts and your minds in Christ Jesus. Finally, brethren, whatever is true, whatever is honorable, whatever is right, whatever is pure, whatever is lovely, whatever is of good repute, if there is any excellence and if anything worthy of praise, dwell on these things."* (Philippians 4:4-8).

Knowing what Paul was facing when he wrote these words changes everything. Understanding that he wrote

Dwell On These Things
(Philippians 4:8)

this in perhaps his darkest sky moment puts real power behind it. Paul was not trying to tell us to have an unrealistic view of the world and just pretend it is all good when it is not. Paul understood that life is hard, extremely hard at times, and the skies get quite dark. But what we choose to focus on in those moments will make all the difference for us.

The Apostle Paul says we can have *a peace from God that transcends or surpasses all understanding.* This means that in the middle of the darkest times in life, when everyone else would seemingly be panicked and riddled with anxiety, we can have this amazing God empowered peace. And Paul says the key to getting this is what we choose to let our mind "dwell" or focus on.

I can tell you from personal experience that putting this into practice can be challenging. When my health takes a turn for the worse as it frequently does with the disease of dysautonomia, my mind seems to naturally dwell on the scary "what ifs". "What if" this gets worse? "What if" this overwhelms me? "What if" this is the beginning of something even more horrible. "What if" this happens or "what if" that happens? This is just naturally where we go. Our skies get darkened and our minds dwell on the various ways that they can potentially get even darker. We must resist this.

To combat the anxiety from the "what ifs" of life, Paul reminded us of four powerful words: *The Lord is near!* God has this. God has us. Whatever the Enemy in this broken world throws at us, God will somehow take us through it. He always has and He always will. Choosing to focus on that can give us peace that transcends all understanding. This is in part why keeping your own pile of rocks that we talked about earlier is so critical. It prevents that God amnesia which causes us to forget that *our Lord is near.*

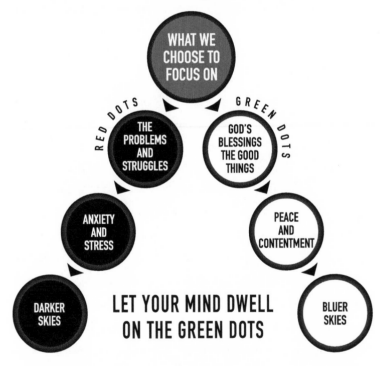

In step 3 of this book we discussed the reality of life in this broken world in that we will always have both those green dots (good stuff) and red dots (bad stuff). But the question becomes which one of those dots are we going to focus on? Focusing our mind on the red dots will lead to anxiety, stress, and depression and will only serve to further darken those skies. When we choose to focus on the green dots and the ways God is still

To combat the anxiety from the "what ifs" of life, Paul reminded us of four powerful words: "The Lord is near!"

blessing us, it can make such a powerful difference.

I do not know what those green dots are in your life. But I do know that God promises to bless His kids. Those green dots are present. However, during dark skies and failing health it can be a mental battle to try to focus our thoughts on them.

I find myself in such a mental battle even as I write these very words. I was just released yesterday from the hospital cardiac monitoring unit. I am suffering from runs of abnormal heart rhythms. The "what ifs" at this moment are frightening for me. "What if" these rhythms won't go away? "What if" my cardiologist needs to perform an invasive and dangerous cardiac ablation to fix it? "What if" I don't survive this? I must tell you every part of my "natural mind" wants to "dwell" on these fears. But, I know that if I continue to "dwell" on this, it will only lead to more anxiety, and to even darker skies. So, as hard as it is right now, I am diligently resisting thinking about the "what ifs" and instead I am reminding myself that my Lord is near and He is still blessing me.

I find myself in such a mental battle even as I write these very words.

We can have peace from God in the middle of the darkest times. The key is what we choose to "dwell" or focus on.

I am instead choosing to focus on those wonderful green dots that are in fact in my life. I am thinking about my wife who loves me and that has been a source of strength for me during this health nightmare. I am thinking about my healthy kids, my awesome church and the people in it who sincerely care for me—these are all amazing blessings from my God Who is near. I look outside and see beautiful trees and mountains off in the distance, and I am reminded of the majesty and the power of my God Who is near. I am petting my devoted dog that warms my heart during struggles such as this, and it again reminds me of the blessings of my God Who is near. I am scared right now . . . of course . . . who wouldn't be? But, I cannot begin to tell you the peace I am feeling as I focus on those wonderful green dots that are a gift from my God Who is near.

So, what about you? What are those green dots that you can be focusing on right now? And I would encourage you to take it one step further—not just focus on those things, but to actually thank God for them. During those dark skies, go to God with an attitude of thankfulness for those green dot blessings.

The most comforting green dot blessing of all is that the Lord is near.

It wasn't just the Apostle Paul who taught us how to find peace in times of tribulation. Jesus Himself told us what we need to be focused on so that we may find peace amid dark skies. He said, *"Peace I leave with you; My peace I give to you; not as the world gives do I give to you. Do not let your heart be troubled, nor let it be fearful."* (John 14:27). So, Jesus tells us that the peace He brings is very different than the peace the world brings. In the world, we can have peace as long as everything is going well. As long as the skies are always blue, then we can have peace. But what happens when our skies turn dark? What happens when the Enemy throws those awful red dots into our lives? Jesus says that is when He steps in and can give us that wonderful, powerful peace. And the key for us to make that happen is to diligently focus our thoughts on those green dot blessings and on Jesus—Who is near!

Author's Prayer

Father,
I am going through a really tough time right now. My
skies seem so dark. The Enemy has put some bad red dots
in my life. But, I know You said that I can have peace in
spite of that. And even though I am hurting right now,
You have blessed me with so many wonderful green
dots in my life . . . and I am so grateful. But, the most
incredible and comforting green dot blessing of all
is that . . . You are near! Thank You my God.
In Jesus' Name, Amen.

R̽ PRESCRIPTION FOR WHEN SKIES AREN'T BLUE

Put these steps into practice daily while you are dealing with difficult times:

1) Actively resist thinking about the red dots in your life and the worrisome "what if" scenarios.

2) Choose to focus on the various green dot blessings from God and thank Him for those things.

3) Draw comfort from the most powerful of all green dot blessings—Jesus is near!

Andy Laurie

ANDY LAURIE, MD

When Skies Aren't Blue

REMEMBER ONE DAY THE SKIES WILL BE ETERNALLY BLUE

I did my medical internship year in 1991. It was by far the most physically and emotionally exhausting experience of my life. This was in an era before there were time restrictions on the number of hours residents could work. It was not uncommon to work over 100 hours per week, including shifts of 36 hours. It was high intensity and high stress work that was exhausting on so many levels. These rotations would last a full month. Interestingly, they would give us a single day "vacation" at the end of the month. This was intentional. Although that one month was miserable, they knew we always looked forward to that day of vacation. Knowing there was going to be a break, albeit a temporary one, was just enough to endure the misery.

We all need hope. The absence of hope is despair. Despair takes an already dark sky and turns it black. The problem so many of us face when dealing with chronic

The absence of hope is despair.

illness is that seemingly there is no hope. The hope that we cling to fades the longer the illness persists. That hope can flat out disappear when we realize that the struggle is an unchangeable one. That certainly is the case for me. I have battled this illness and the suffering for nearly two decades. It is not going away. I know that. So, where is the hope? Where is the hope knowing that I am going to wake up sick every single morning? How can that not lead to despair? Where is that vacation to look forward to?

When we are dealing with those seemingly unchangeable dark sky times in life, we cannot just kind of wish God's promises are true, we need to know. That is why it is so critical that we understand God's promises in the Bible are provable and true. So, what are God's provable promises for those seemingly unchangeable dark-sky moments?

Throughout the entirety of scripture, God is constantly challenging us to discern between the temporary life in this broken world and the promise of a perfect eternity. Jesus frequently pointed to the promises of the perfect world to come. In fact, He tells us straight up not to *"store up treasures on earth where moth and rust destroy and thieves break in and steal"*. Instead, He implores us to store up those *"treasures in heaven"* (Matthew 6:19-21). He is challenging us to think eternally. The Apostle Paul tells us that, *"flesh and blood cannot inherit the kingdom of God, nor does the perishable inherit the imperishable"* (1 Corinthians 15:50). The very theme of the book of Revelation is that this temporary, broken world is destined to perish and ultimately will be replaced by an eternally perfect one.

In fact, in a bigger sense the entire Bible is God's plan of transforming eternity lost in Eden to paradise gained forever through Christ. God could not be any clearer. He wants us to understand that this world is broken. It is temporary. It is *not* our final home. And for our peace, contentment and ultimately for our enduring hope, He wants us to keep our sights on the eternal home which will be perfect in every way—where the sky is always blue!

Keeping our focus on our final home where the sky is always going to be blue takes work. It does not come naturally. Our natural tendency is to *God challenges us to discern between the temporary life in this broken world and the promise of a perfect eternity.* dwell on the negative and the darkness. We must actively combat this. As I struggle with poor health, I constantly remind myself that this is temporary. When the nausea is overwhelming, I remind myself there will come a time that I will be feasting in heaven. When my physical body is worn down and suffering, I remind myself that my eternal body will be perfect in every way. When sleep seems to be the only escape from this crummy illness, I must think of the amazing final dawn where the light of God will illuminate everything with its perfection forever.

This is not just some new age power of positive thought. It is provable truth. All our suffering will come to an end. And then there will be perfection, forever. It is real.

It is a fact. And it is the enduring hope that I cling to even in the darkest days of this seemingly unchangeable illness.

I regularly remind myself that this body which is suffering is not my final body. In fact, every afternoon I have programmed my phone to pop up a scripture that reminds me of this. It is 2 Corinthians 4:16 which says, *"Therefore we do not lose heart, but though our outer man is decaying, yet our inner man is being renewed day by day."*

Our natural tendency is to dwell on the negative and the darkness. We must actively combat this.

I talk to God about this in my prayers. God reminds me in those prayers that the real *me* is not this outward body which is sick and suffering and wearing out. But the real *me* is strong, healthy and beautiful, and made in the image of my Creator. Regardless of how crummy my outer man/ body is feeling, God is continuously making that inner man stronger and healthier day by day. My life is not winding down in sickness and weakness. But it is gaining momentum each day as I draw closer to that amazing time when I will be home with my Lord in perfection, forever.

I know this may sound kind of odd. But I do something on those awful health days that really does help me. When I am really suffering, I literally look right back at my body and tell it that you are not me. The real me is within and made in God's image. And it is healthy, and it is strong, and it is renewing and revving up to that amazing day when it will be home forever in perfection.

This may sound fatalistic and depressing. It is not. It is

an appropriate and mentally healthy way to look at life. I am not desiring my own death. I cherish the gift of life God has given me, and

I regularly remind myself that this body which is suffering is not my final body.

I strive to the best of my ability to make the most of it. I fully intend to try and impact my world for Jesus in the most effective way possible. But I have learned to endure these rough, dark sky moments by keeping my focus on the reality that this is not my final home, and this is not my final body. This suffering is temporary.

ETERNAL TAPE MEASURE

In fact, when it comes to the temporary nature of our suffering, I like to view life through the "eternal tape measure." Imagine, if you will, a tape measure. Now let us pretend that this tape measure represents our *life*. But here is the kicker, only the first inch represents our earthly life. Everything that happens to us in this body on this planet occurs in that first inch. We are physically born, we grow up, we go to school, we have our first love, we get married, we have kids, we work and retire. That all happens in that first inch. And yes, in that first inch we feel pain and we suffer, and we get sick and eventually our physical bodies die. And that all happens in that first inch of the *eternal tape measure*.

But what happens after our body dies? Well, we then spend the rest of our *life* in our new home with our new bodies. It will be perfect in every way. Guess what? That portion of the tape measure goes on and on and on. It is without end.

Now let us put suffering in that perspective. The time that we suffer and go through those dark sky moments is but a tiny mark on the *eternal tape measure*. We tend to think that this life and this world and these bodies are everything. But in fact, they are inconsequentially small compared to the tape measure which goes on forever. Because of that, we can endure. We put our focus not on the suffering blip on the timeline of our earthly life. Instead, we keep our mind on the enduring eternally blue skies of our final home with God.

The time that we suffer and go through those dark sky moments is but a tiny mark on the eternal tape measure.

It is this eternal home with God that we are to keep our focus on. Even though we are not there yet, just the hope of that home will brighten even the darkest skies. In a fascinating exchange between Jesus and His disciples in John 14, Jesus started talking to them about this eternal home. I suspect that many of the descriptions of this amazing place were not recorded. But suffice to say, it was no doubt incredible enough that the disciples asked the obvious question: *What is the way to get to this home?* Jesus responded in what may be one of the most famous passages in the entire Bible, *"I am the WAY and the truth and the life and no one comes to the Father but through Me."* (John 14:6).

It is only through Christ that we may spend our eternity with our Father in that amazing home— where the skies are forever blue!

Author's Prayer

Father,
It sometimes gets me down knowing that I am likely
going to spend the rest of my life feeling this crummy.
But Father, I can be strong through this because I know
full well that this suffering is temporary. I know this
world is not my final home. And I know that when all is
said and done, I will be with You in that incredible place
where it will be perfect in every way—where the skies
will always be blue.
In Jesus' Name, Amen.

Rx PRESCRIPTION FOR WHEN SKIES AREN'T BLUE

Take these important steps this week:

1) Envision your life as that eternal tape measure.

2) Picture your current struggle as a tiny blip within that first inch.

3) Let it give you peace, knowing your life will be eventually perfect for the remainder of that eternal tape measure.

4) Thank God for sending Jesus as the Way to that eternal perfection.

Andy Laurie

ANDY LAURIE, MD

ABOUT THE AUTHOR

Andy and Cyndi, 2020

Doctor Andy Laurie is a board-certified radiologist who received his medical degree from UC San Diego. He did his post graduate residency at the University of Arizona. He practiced emergency radiology for nearly thirty years before illness caused him to recently retire. In addition, he has been a pastor at The Bridge Christian Church in Tucson, Arizona, for nearly twenty years. For much of this time, he has courageously battled a devastating disease of the autonomic nervous system. Doctor Laurie and his wife, Cyndi, were married in 1991 after he graduated from medical school. They have four grown children and make their home in Tucson with their beloved dogs!

Family Gathering 2020

Made in United States
Orlando, FL
02 September 2022

21890894R00071